BESIDE
OURSELVES

The Miami University Press Poetry Series
General Editor: James Reiss

BESIDE OURSELVES

POEMS BY NANCE VAN WINCKEL

Miami University Press
Oxford, Ohio

Library of Congress Cataloging-in-Publication Data

Van Winckel, Nance.
    Beside Ourselves / Nance Van Winckel
        p. cm.
        ISBN 1-881163-43-1 (alk. paper) -- ISBN 1-881163-44-X (alk. paper)
        I. Title.
    PS3554.R83 B87 2003
    811'.54--dc21
2002070924

The paper in this book meets the guidelines
for permanence and durability of the Committee
on Production Guidelines for Book Longevity
of the Council on Library Resources. ∞

Printed in the U.S.A.

9 8 7 6 5 4 3 2 1

ACKNOWLEDGMENTS

Thanks to the editors of these journals in which the following poems—some in slightly different versions—first appeared:

Ascent: "Dear Compatriots"

The Beloit Poetry Journal: "Mission Creep"

Colorado Review: "No?"

Crazyhorse: "The Answering" and "Suddenly a New Way"

Field: "At the Higher Elevations," "Everything Falls Away," "The Party Men in the Perfumery," and "Taking it Home"

Gettysburg Review: "Getting In" and "Happier Horses"

Grand Street: "He Wants"

High Plains Literary Review: "The Gathering," "Always Too Much and Never Enough," and "Late Fall"

The Journal: "Black Ledgers"

The Kenyon Review: "Celsius" and "These Days"

The Massachusetts Review: "Jump Shift"

Michigan Quarterly Review: "Mistakes" and "Clown with Black Wings"

The Paris Review: "Threshold"

Poetry Miscellany: "The Unseen Buttresses Upon Which Heaven Rests"

The Seneca Review: "Watching the Men Walk" and "What?"

Third Coast: "Of No Matter"

The Virginia Quarterly Review: "Envoys" and "If You're Happy & You Know It"

West Branch: "Cautionary Tale," "To the Far North," and "Whoever's the Last Blessed Blows Out the Candle"

Also, thanks to the National Endowment for the Arts whose support in the form of a 2001 Poetry Fellowship helped toward the completion of this book.

"A Danube Suite" owes much to Charles Wright, and the last two lines of Section IV are from Wright's "The Southern Cross," p. 48, *The World of the Ten Thousand Things* (New York: Farrar, Straus & Giroux, 1990). Also, many thanks to Karen Seashore for parts of "Dear Compatriots."

CONTENTS

. . . the horses
Rattled the empty chariots through the fields of battle,
Longing for their noble drivers. But they on the ground
Lay, dearer to the vultures than to their wives.

—Homer, *The Iliad*
(translated by Mary McCarthy with Dwight MacDonald)

I

The Alarming Suddenness of the Provisional

The poplars laid their long shadows
across the sunken belly of the pond.
Patrol cars sat empty in Karolivov Park.
Police on corners with sugary fingers
from crullers and souvlaki. Music
from mouth-harps and mandolins,

while the bakery across the park sparked
and burned. Into perpetuity. A greasy
ashy smoke. Hydrants busted, hoses
out of water. The flare-up and die-down
of the flame. And the pond licking back
at its shadows—an immanence, a sheen.

The cross-legged musicians played bluegrass
from my country—a foreign happiness
to accompany the reign of cinders
and platters of pastries set out on the green.
The precipitate crowd, devouring every
morsel, kept time with their toes.

MISSION CREEP

Shuffle twice and deal. Let poker deliver us
down the ten cold steps to morning. Too much blood
in the river turns it dark. Disembodied and disremembered,
what does a dead corporal recall of his old orders?
Not a word, not a glyph in the moonlight.

The greened-out countryside hurt our eyes
after hours around a table,
talking the bones of our faces dry. The work
asked only a small piece of me—that was *it*
to transport the words across the worlds.

Shush. Say nothing of import. Little ears
overhear. The boys finger their coins
and ante up. Vodka for verve. Dawn lightens
the river's load. From its shimmer a hand
is raised. It calls and I see, too far gone to fold.

THE GATHERING

An old woman ties the dead man's shoes.
Two girls pick through pebbles, make a ridge of them
around his ankles. Standing next to his shoulders,
three boys examine a fourth boy's scar—a missing
thumb. The dead man's radio plays a song
from the southern province. Tambourines
and trumpets rattling the windows
of duct-taped glass on a tipped building—

across the street from where we watch as another
even older woman arrives, squats by the body
and begins shelling peas into a glass jar.

Finally the officer—stern and pressed—
appears, stares at the dead man, then turns,
snapping our picture just as we snap his.

SPIDERS

One finger against his lips. His eyes
swept the ceiling. *Bugged.* The car too.
Our dinner table, elevator, hallway.

Spiders, he whispered once, *everywhere.*
Someone, please say something. We're all
tired. We've stood lookout too long.

And he and I—two tight knots
far apart on a thin rope. Not to say it
but to hear it all the time, scratching.

The rope drags. Catches on chairs. Charades
and finger-talk. His hand on my arm
half out a car door. *What? What?*

Syllables fall, the rope drags. And something
crawls the walls with our names in its mouth,
tongue-tied and scratching, scratching.

WILD, ONE-EYED JACKS

Downstairs, loaves of bread breathe in the air for us
and grow. Sunup's purple has rubbed off on my arms.

Hold, hold, hold. Poker—five hands open
and face down on morning's cold first step.

A man's fist from yesterday echoes off a table. Saying
his words were God's, so by-god get them right.

Clink, clink: call and hold. Stacks of coins our boys
don't know the names of. Three of these and two of those.

Mice in the walls, dogs at the door.
And under holy edicts that no woman should be able

to utter, the thousand-year-old daggers fly skyward—
and not a single fire yet lit in the village.

Late Fall

Don't look down, you said. Far off,
farmers with flashlights turned their fields.
The plows seemed to pull the horses on.
Soon a dust would liven up the dawn.
I'd paint eyes on eyes. To stare
into the grit. To walk against the sky.

It was not so high a building. Your hand
on my arm. My black slip, cool as the hoped-for storm,
still concealed. You stepped back from the edge,
shaking your head. No. Not to look.

Later, alone, I saw the black straps fall
in the mirror. My feet in that dark pool, you
miles away up the hall, and finally the rain
overhead, hard as a hundred hooves.

Negative Operability

We need some music
to repair us, I said to the men
whose mission was to get
from worst to only mildly
bad. All right, yes, two swigs
on the straight-away
before the border check. Long
cello notes against the tire-whir.
God's a wiseacre, the violin swears
whenever it's allowed.

Here, stop. One man pissing
behind the car. Another shouts
out the window into the rococo
leaf-splay around the bloodwort
to Watch it, watch your back.

No?

Last night we stood a long time on the roof.
The movie in the village over, and still
its sadness. From the film, the lovers' faces
kept advancing. Past the belltower's two clocks—
neither ticking the right time. Past
the girl in the square who'd said
she wanted to paint my nails blue:
A blue on you is young, no?

Downstairs, our rooms waited. Distant
beds. And farther off: that double-faced
clock: clown and saint. Luminous.
Your eyes on my slight touch: blue
fingertips against the red knot of your tie.

In the film the lovers' punishment
was the heartsickness of their children:
alone, adrift on a shore fouled by dead
herring. Dropping off, I saw them again—
faces flushed, the boy and girl clearing a stretch
of beach, heaving putrid fish on a mound
growing higher and higher.

TAKING IT HOME

A woman carrying a window
on her back. Passersby clear a path

to let her through. But no—each by each,
they aim to fall in behind, to see and be seen
by the glass: sublimely kind today.

Down the street, approaching the stone bridge,
the woman's steps get slower, deeper, heavier.

The Unseen Buttresses Upon Which Heaven Rests

The stoned bellboys stagger
across the marble floors. Yank at
and laugh at the wobbly wheeled bags
as if they're disobedient pups.
Outside the Novotel Imperiàl, a miracle
when the fog lifts. Some vault of the dead
opened. The boys follow our line of vision
to the sun. Eastward: the Bay of Birds,
hunched divot of the Black Sea.

Just last week the boys were waiters.
Their purple uniforms—gold-tasseled now—
still emanate an odor of salami and eggs,
of singed grass and summery sweet absinthe.
We breathe them in, these boys
with the breaths of children, full
of their own apocryphal histories—
hopeless and corrupt, as ours are.
The glare of light stuns us. One by one,
we slip on our new black-market sunglasses
to see into it: the future, the grandeur.

II

ENVOYS

You asked about the slogans on the platform's
posters: black X's across jaundiced faces, what
the red type said. We'd just stepped off the train
into one more town briefly without rulers.

Only snow. The old consonant-heavy language
felt like soot in my mouth. The locals shrugged
and looked away, embarrassed. My hands flailing
in confettied air. To have touched you then

would have brought the snow down harder
on the land of anarchy. At last someone pointed us
to the inn, where we didn't have the right money
but no one cared. No one had. Inside, on a table
lay dozens of wet wool gloves—all palms up,
dripping, their frozen gestures thawing.

SUDDENLY A NEW WAY

The planes overhead were from a friendly
country. You couldn't say which one.
You'd said too much already.

It's one more brown eraser smudge
on your map—when the river washes out
the dirt road we've come in on.

In suddenly a new way the river dredges
another bed. Takes down a shed, two beech trees,
a mule. It has, the leek farmer says,
done this for goddamn ever.

When the next, smaller planes
flew past, you frowned. Said nothing.

You and I had lived our lives a continent
apart—years inside other marriages
and a quasi-peace of passed platters, gravies, goblets.

The water was a filthy, bubbling mud.
The farmer buckled his waders and slogged out
into it, tugged at and finally jerked loose
a stuck cage of drowned somethings—animals
he had to explain three times
were rabbits, before we got it.

THE GOODS

Squatting for hours over the items
to be sold, and not thinking once
about them. Not really crossing his
ten-year-old mind: that box of kitchen knives.

He's only the middle man.
Middle son on a middle street. Even
opening the box to show me, he won't
look inside. Where nothing shines.

Nothing is sharp. Extinct tools
to a people whose pigs are all dead.
Who stare through the steam of one yellow turnip
cooked to oblivion in a black pot.

GETTING IN

My earring caught on your coat sleeve as we ducked
into the cab. Then your slow careful unsnagging.
The one waiter in the town's only restaurant
had apologized for offering only a single entree,
but it was good—venison poached from across the river.

Later the thickening rain, and the driver going
too fast. Close quarters in the backseat
and my face leaning in to your hand
as it pulled my gold hoop loose—My fishhooks,
I said, and I'm sorry, it's my fault.

The taxi's tight turn, and the driver's Whoops,
and No, it's me, you said, I'm clumsy.
Rain-flooded streets pooling against the tires.
Softly your breath and mouth on my name,
on my lips. Pausing there. And sitting back

in it then, the wet around us as we stared
straight ahead. And no one saying Sorry,
not even the driver who'd missed our street,
turned—skidding, backtracking, cursing—
half-lost in his own town in the downpour.

THE GIST OF THE MISSION

Gold mosque domes and stone aqueducts from 1200.
No shadows, and the hot white ghosts of noon.
Chalked letters down the side of a charred building
a block from the soldiers' cemetery, and her squinting,
telling them she couldn't see, so as not to have to say
they'd been sworn back into the dogs who'd borne them.

Sometimes there's a general inquiry about the States,
but no one has any idea that on her road out West,
men, who carry just a burlap sack and a stick,
collect rattlesnakes. No man who's done this
hasn't been bit. Ask and you'll be shown the double
drilled holes, the hard places that never soften.

What's bagged in back of a pick-up writhes. Soon
to be serum. To be antidote to what they do.

In the Early Days of Our Love,

he awoke and said that in his dream
he'd been praying in a corner of the chamber
when a man stepped in—a technician
who couldn't make the gas come on.

His black boots loud on the white tiles.
He pushed a path through the consigned ones
in order to tap on then pound the pipes.
It's no use, he told them. Disgusted.

Stomping out, he didn't bother closing
the chamber doors, so everyone came and stood
just inside the threshold, staring down the road.
Distant billowing trees. The jeep speeding off,

and its radio antenna bobbing on back
with the small crimson flag no one could stop
watching—even when it was merely
after-image, a red dot in the dust.

THRESHOLD

All this rain in the place where it rarely rains.
Eyes trained on the sky as if for smoke,
as if for news of the next doddering pope.

It always comes down to God. To God
and money. At cross-purposes across borders
penciled in: rain-blurred on a back seat.

Balkan backlighting over a valley of bad roads
driven too fast to get through. Pencil lines.
Treaties that last two days or two hours.

What lasted a week last week: the export
of low-grade silver, an exchange of embassies.
What is finally the fireflies' was first the roses'.

What a woman knew better than to do, she did.
Worlds of rock and sand, across which
she walked barefoot by the Black Sea.

And so bruised her foot on a rock. Blue
across the instep. A man kneeling over it.
His finger tentative above its arc.

Worn-down flesh that's never been kissed
is kissed. The valley's light is ground fine and
tuned low. Blue doors open to blue rooms.

Balconies buoy up the robed men
and gowned women. They lift bare arms
over the rails to receive the shock of the shower.

Its joy and musical cascade collect
in the bruised cheek of sunset.
No sky can contain so much plunder.

Sweetheart, he'd whispered when the blue
struck him. That calling . . . that touching
were the lengths to which, lame as she was,

she felt summoned to meet what shouldn't
be met. The obligatory translation of which
will some day come down to *rock*—it was

a small one, they'll say, sun-warmed
and pressed up into the curve of flesh
that slipped down on it.

The Party Men in the Perfumery

They've broken men's fingers to get where
they are. An easy job like this. Here
to make a last inspection and lock
the doors. But dizzy when they do. Attar of roses—
once the prime export—its aged sweetness
smacking their eyes shut. Room
to room, a hurt that hobbles them,
breathless past the cold copper vats.

CALL TO ORDER

All-night negotiation. In the hotel lobby
guards doze near the flickering TV,
its bla-bla-blustering voice offering statues

of infant saints. Around us, a fishy air
and the windows painted shut. Outside,
it's the rat-and-cat-thick city and someone fiddling
with a radio, tuning in wails and spit.

In my country it was good once to stick
a fish face and three seeds of corn in a hill.
Sweet when a rain whispered down.

I lift my head from my arms
around this dream. Time now to repeal
what ripples wild out of me
and toward the man who drops the gavel.

Red finch wings dart off behind my eyes.
The man's arm, striking the tap-tap-tap,
knocks the dregs of a short rest back.

WHAT?

Two sides of the same sky: so we don't know
where to look. Left: to the stooped back of the storm.
Right, where the sunny sweetness drains down.

And the two of us swirled away an hour ago
on a blanket red as Moses's robe. So wake now.

Wake up before the dark and light close in. A crank
wound on a vise. One mouth puts its loneliness
all over another's. A whir behind the winding.

What used to be God pushes on both sides at once. West:
in grimy undershirts, understudies for the leading clouds.

East: the sun's ache. A posit and a praxis. The sky's seam
loosens. Up here the knoll doesn't want us—hence its bulge
to throw us off. The ripped robe of Prometheus drags us.

The seam splits. We've heard it before but never listened
as we do now. The world makes us listen.

What was formerly called love is this silence
around our staring: after kissing, after the sound of it
seeps down and makes ulcers in the heart.

At the western edge of my homeland, the new-age brain
is burning: hard, bituminous. And the young bodies,
thickly greased against all rays of it, ride it along.

What used to be us looks for a verb for us. Sick of the noun
of us. What was me: commas, brackets, dashes. Blots and blotches.

Your French by way of the bald man's Bulgarian, via my
Russian torqued into English, and *What?* Qu´est-ce que c´est?

We ride the red robe over a hill. Sky eating sky, the village
gets the deluge first. Soon we'll have to go back
down there, and have our story straight.

The sigh that's left of you utters itself thoroughly and clearly
into me—the me of cool parenthesis, clean
and hammered far apart by this rain.

WHAT NEXT?

Our driver writes love letters to two women
at once. Carefully not saying the same thing
twice. The moon gleams, or the sea does.

This girl's downy arms, the other one's eyes
a blue fog . . . . He holds a pencil by its black lead.
Chiseled letters, erasures, sighs.

He strings his tongue up a tower—hot and red.
Hard words make him squint and stare. High sun
over the dash on this untoward present tense,

where I follow back behind the verbiage, beneath
the tight-stitched rhyme. He smiles at the paper.
A gold-toothed and complaining wind, he catches

my eye in the mirror, but he won't take
my help. Says Nope: these days, this lifetime,
he must make more of himself.

These Days

In the mausoleum lies the corpse of a man who rode
in a black limo, burgundy velvet over the windows,
who drank grape brandy and griped about his liver,
griped about Nomenklatura and all manner of ass-
kissing in the party, though before he was dead, he was
the party, dying by slow degrees from Stalin's poison.

Four decades under glass. Never a Perestroika man.
Face and fingers spectrally lit. The yellow streetlights
come on for an hour, then off for two. Lignite smoke
browning the day's fresh snow. Because you asked me to,
I put on black boots, stood by the cavernous body
in formaldehyde. Four degrees under a freeze.

Down chipped cobblestones, we'd crossed a glaze of snow.
Though the body beside me spoke with your voice, its hands
hardly seemed yours touching the glass. Our oval sighs of breath
blasted beside a week's worth of new graffiti: what could be,
what should be, shoved inside the dead man's orifices.
And no one paid these days to paint it over.

Black Ledgers

On the snowy shore Army boys
shoot blanks at bales of hay.

Through the eye of our scope, tanks
rolling in. The one who looks
must count. *Thirteen, fourteen* . . .
his job makes him sigh. *Fifteen*. He blinks,
he looks. He can't see. He can't think.

A welder's bead burns ice blue dots
down the ship's prow.

Odors from below: fried blackfish. Liver.
Snails. Cooked tongue. St. Anthony hangs
in the mess. The captain awaiting notes

and deck-boys on the run. Stamping up
narrow stairs, then back down. To the dark cave
of caged ivory chickens. More counting, but
backwards this time as heads swagger off.

The chickens make a noise like thunder
when the boy throws open the door.

Amorphous Borders

A stork rose from the sewer reservoir, flapping,
dragging her stick legs—just as our train crossed the river
between two countries and its heater shut down.

Never pausing from their prayers, two women
kicked off their white sling-back shoes, bent,
and wrapped their feet in black wool scarves.

One shows the other a tiny Christ from a kiosk
at the last station. They run their fingers
over his silver tacks, the shiny stigmata.

When the train lights flickered off, the women set down
the Christ and put their heads back. As I did.
In the seat beside me a man was asleep, his breathing

slow as the stork's wings, which kept on and kept on.
My town on the back side of this world must have been
waking: that yeast smell in the steam, the beer and the bread.

Once the ones who lived there sold their whole lake
for iron muskrat traps and happier horses. They sang the name
of the water so the fish would stay: *Il-Lae-Loo. Lake Il-Lae-Loo.*

Dusk, and that singing on the dock. My grandfather's
hired boys lopping off fish heads, singing.
Lake Michigan cold and the deerflies nipping.

The heat clicks on and clicks off. A cloud-bank swallows
the bird's soup-pot jowls. The man's hand drifts,
slips beneath the coat on my lap, as we cross

the same river into yet another country—this one
a good one, with a lit station and American rock music
blasted as we hurtle past—pulled on and pulled on.

A savior dozes between two women. When last
he woke, it was the zero century, and he was a boy
cracking sticks on the street. The ride to the end a blink.

Blink, and this sleep is a pebble carried in the great
gullet of the dream—augering down the lava core
and rising into the night mountains, over them, towards

the Black Sea, and into the station there still unlit
when the women wake, startled, and have to hurry,
carrying their white shoes down the steps into the dark.

HAPPIER HORSES

What holds their bones together
pours past me. Four frail ankles
under each great girth. A steady pounding
against the earth's chest: Hurry,
open up, come out.

Cool roan hemispheres, measure me,
empty me, pass me on.

Because someone misheard me. Someone
whose gauge of English was a dropped clock
from 1800. Heard me say I was a *rider,*
not a *writer*—and had his driver
take me to his private stables.

The horses there bored and half-wild
from neglect. Breaths of a meadow,
eyes of old wine and new jewels.
The driver stepping away
to say, Now didn't I tell you,
a sweet surprise, no?

All of him dismissing me
to the saddle that had already been set high
like a fire—fixed and red hot. Then up
and into it, where the wind is galvanic.
Is ours. Where the horizon edges closer
and we're about to leap over
the gate of it: to honeyed cloud-bales,
sweet manna of the terra infirma.

THE ANSWERING

If there's anything sour in him, it must be her.
He listens inside himself for a ringing, the answering
to which his virtue begs questions.

The hotel is a distant chatter of birds. Dark
balustrades to which they fly and depart.
His chest rises and falls, and my ear listens there.

And though the listening drifts now, it will wake
when a call comes. Whatever he promised her
will be the echo around the call,

so I'll have to go stand outside on the balcony
and let the cold wind blow through my robe
so as *not* to hear. The ringing is the lingo—

instructions pinged through the wires. It's excess
questions he can't answer. When anything hurts
in him, it turns him over. The body asleep

but listening for a waking. The hand receives.
It hears. It lifts and sifts the silence. Enunciates the lies.
It prepares the room to be a ghost of this ringing.

FEEDING THE LIE

Having told only small ones. A dead mouse in the basement
I said I hadn't seen. The next week another.
And my husband picking them up by their tails.

The village's curtains are yanked up, and I rehearse
my monologue against the dark window. Implications of
my nipples in another man's mouth. Audience
of Carpathian Mountains in snow-laced yarmulkes.

Back-lit and back-stage, it loomed up from years ago
when I'd lifted the garbage lid, dropped in a piece
of white cake—bubbled green from weeks in the fridge—
that largeness inside the steel drum, rank and
undeniable as the pink tail, as the fetal
crouch around tiny clawed feet.

OF NO MATTER

The Little Sisters of Saint Teresa bring back
full flasks from the river, laughing, flicking
water on each other. It's all right
since the jugs have not yet been blessed
and the water inside is still icy
from the deepest eddies. Yes, bring on
the vespers. Walk us a few steps
nearer the happy ones on the footbridge,
while the priest continues napping.
By the time he blesses that water,
it will be warmed through
by the girls' laughter. So it's of no matter
if we take off our shoes and stand awhile
in the current. The girls' husband is everywhere
and nowhere. On and off, the sunlight of wedlock
strikes their gold bands, marries them
and unmarries them from the river.

III

A Danube Suite

A Danube Suite

I. Goodbye

Along the banks the farmers' pumpkins scoff.
Taunting skulls, fattened on the water's one-word line,
which the river's rehearsed—hell-bent on a perfect
delivery—but never gets to say.

Ships from the Ukraine bring pig iron
and coal to feed the blast furnaces. Cows
pass on the banks, aimed toward a warm barn.
The boy behind them looks up at the sky
as if up a girl's skirt. Black. Organza.

And someone watching from a hotel window.
How sweet the error of her ways. Joy
shoving back at shame. On the dresser,
a century-old candle, and her thumbnail-rub
for the smell: the old world stubbed, God
coughing from the bluffs. The monastery up there
laid open by cannonballs ten tyrants ago,
the fire-power launched from here—right here
where she's standing, wind-burned and gin-soaked,
wasted in the wee hours.

II. From Our Side

The foreign girls are pretty and sad
and off-limits. And like it
that way—there
on their side. Waving
hankies. Each girl each day
in a different dress.

In the chapel yesterday, the priest's one hand
touching a woman's head, the other
trying to lay a wafer on her tongue—trying and failing
and passing on. Mist and the awkwardness
of the spirit. Godly ideas in the rain,
mother-of-pearl light through the Sunday paper,
and a slug creeps out from the heart.

Over there: the thin-skinned baltas,
buttressed by marshes. And the spoonbills
nesting around the fortress, now the island's
labor camp, where, for the guards' amusement,
rapists have their way with the party insurgents.

Hydrofoils of tourists gun up and slow down
for pictures: the heavy-bellied birds high up
on the ancient ramparts.

III. Spent But Also Saved

The sky's sinewy blue torso.
White tattoos needled in. Such
machismo. That steely-eyed stare. No
pain. Feeling no pain.

Two fingers poured over ice
stays on her mind—that
beside the day's duties. Numbered
and lettered. Columnar. The burn of river
past her window, and nothing to dowse its fire.

Through the glue of girlhood—that gold light
poured out and fanned out. To rappel down
its viscous plume, sticky with pond bugs, paper
doll dresses, firecracker wrappers. . . .

Sky palm over its own mouth. Sparklers
of ash now, and hush, hush.

IV. Black Organza

She remembers when she could forget herself, one
hand on her hip, and the rest of her
let Go. Days of Gone. Montana's Mission Mountains
blinking on, off. Because they can. The all-there
of them. The mission to surround
the Gone. A whir, and . . . a blink-blink.

Yet hard tonight to recall exactly how the snow
dusted the mountains' open jaws. Stroked on
the opalescence. Some. . . kind of . . . softness . . . .

The river trudges through. Susurrous
about going. The mouth with its mauve lips
hanging open. Wordless. Mouth in the Far Below.
Wet grass that just was, then wasn't beneath her feet.

And ha!—those Crusaders. Dots of their campsites
every few miles along the banks.
Their feet dangled in the water. Tired, so tired
from their long party trip, taking with them
the best wine, fattened pigs, cakes. . . .

The river blinks and swirls. Long ago,
in her stiff party dress, she took the hand of a poet,
was swung out and abandoned—there
inside the spin and his gentleman's reminder, *Don't,
don't forget: everyone's life is the same life
if you live long enough.*

V. Second Person

Lawless steppe: desolate and hurled north
around the Black Sea. The eye of August closing,
but the eyebrow arched. The hand of the image
in its glove of sound—to enter its flippant wave
at the *you*. Down where the river resides.
From the first droplet, having bequeathed its I.

Her husband's long stride across the back field
back home. New-mowed. The starlings crazy
behind him, hurrying him out of their way
so they can have the insect dregs to themselves.
His face dust-streaked. His cap low. Twenty
thousand miles away—his walk. His walk.

The spherule of river swells. Into you. Then it's
its own presence. Its own ache. It: made from
a disappeared I and you, a 1 and a 2, that bloom
of waltzes. Courteous music for courtiers.

VI. Leo, Leo Minor, and the Sextans

The centuries' bite has made the Carpathians serene—inured
to dazzle and drift. The river's storyline long discussed,
then dismissed. Dissolved. Fish gums gnaw it to nothing.

On the bank cattle egrets hover over their beloveds. Hover
and descend. Taste and flight. A wash of rain
and a little phlegm from God's diseased lung.

The river fills and grinds down. Picking up childhoods
as it goes, gurgling them through the plumes
of the refinery's sulfurous ablutions. The water trying

to tell its tale to the scribes overhead, who are sweet
and well-meaning and dyslexic and nuts,
hunching the letters in a backwards script.

VII. No Amends

No declensions in this world for that person. Third. Who's
seen but not heard. Who has much to say.

Sky-palm over the river's mouth. Hush.
If emptiness is the beginning, fullness is the end.

Up there, young stars already in a hurry for the fizz
and go. Whomp and gone. Gold decline down

the lush décolletage, this sweet valley
through which the river drools its sweat.

Twenty-thousand miles off, the hummingbird
sucking the sweetness out of a red or yellow this or that.

Red bandanna on someone's head as she pulls a weed, flutter-
hum by her ears. She freezes. Eye to eye, who's fooling

whom? Needle-beak in her hugely ornamented hair—
she's his wondrous blossom, full of nothing.

VIII. Gin and the Other Five Senses

Beneath the river is its own glossary of secondary meanings.
No *one* ripples the page. The surface stays still. Goodbye
is the plank those who want to die
walk out on. Standing there because they have no
weight, and because the breath of water buoys them.

The Byzantine diplomats thought they knew this.
Unctuously tender to the barbarians. To turn them
back beyond the bluffs. Followed by the long
ha-ha. Ha, ha, history's hilarious.

The river wills the rest of the world supine.
Since it is. Gin and the other five senses set back
on their haunches. Even the synapses of fucking—
frozen, crystallized till the fog passes. Diesel rigs up
on the switchbacks rev and go, rev and gone.

Stag-head of stars, nod once
if you hear, twice if you know the way.

IV

THE AVANT-GARDE

Behind a railcar warehouse, the bronze Lenins
with busted noses, missing chunks of feet. Ice
and pigeon shit on chipped mustaches. Five
headless torsos leaning every way at once.

And a girl tying one end of a jumprope
to half a hand. Taking her time. Looping
a noose up and over, testing the cinch,
her whole face the size of the halved palm.

She picks up her end. Gives it a few
slow turns. By her feet a pocked bronze eye
stares into the sun. She steps back a step.
Turns faster. Getting the right torque.

So all is perfected, though the day's still early,
the school bell not yet rung. The girl studies
the spin, whomps up the beat, already lost,
already singing what must be sung.

If You're Happy & You Know It

A man and a woman on the window's
glass. He touches her hair, tips
her chin. *Just look at them,* I said.
Who do they look like?

He whispers in her ear. *Lovers,*
you said. *They look like lovers.*
They are gray on the black glass.
Adrift into a kiss. They are us.

Below: shoestrings of light tangling
the strung-out city. People living off
angers, eons-old. Fishing the pools
of it. Thin, mercury-pinked smelt.

He and she unbuttoning each other's
shirts, unable to bear their own bliss,
their quiet inside the chaos. Overhead
a great soaring engine roars

and the window rattles, and we
resist ourselves as we are,
as they are, trembling
there on the glass.

MERCILESS BLESSINGS

The church steps were full of amputees
and peddlers selling apples I'd found
were mostly worms at the core.

Weeping, widows walked up and down, going in
to light candles or weep louder before a priest.

A first spring day and still hours
from curfew. Suddenly a stump
held up its bouquet of ballpoint pens.
We winced when we looked down . . . must be
some sort of hole in the wrist.

Orphans took our coins and let us pass.
They fed their monkey vodka
and it danced. An organ ground out a song.

And once again in a passing limo
the city shifted its allegiance.

CLOWN WITH BLACK WINGS

His mop of red hair. Starched wings.
Wearing two costumes at once. Funny
and holy. Cross-dressing. Crossing
Prince Street against the traffic.
Getting halfway on his big white feet.

For an hour we were out of the dream.
Your fingers around a cup of black tea.
From the café we watched the weather (hard rain)
and the politics (chaos) distill into this figure
taxi drivers veered around—honking, fist-shaking.

At his back two crinoline wings the wind inflated
as if to take him up, but for those long white feet,
befuddled now, what with the parade so far
off course—the devils, the dwarves, the dancing
Lippazaners—way over near Checkpoint Nine.

CHECKPOINT NINE

The guard stabs out a cigarette
on our bumper. A drizzle of sparks
between the headlights. I bear witness,
pass the passports, repeat an answer
before the question's asked. Tap-tap of flashlight
against our windshield and your hand
brushing mine on the car seat
so the driver won't see, but he does. Off
down a bad road. Among its borders
of blue corn flowers, now and then
a green patina of the claymores.

MISTAKES

The taxis veering around the clown were empty
but for their drivers whose salaries were paid
whether they picked up fares, or not. Such
was the old system of rule. In its last days.
Army uniforms filthy, even the red suspenders.

In the capital people were eating their pets. Crying
and eating. So explained the TV woman.
Then she turned the viewers' attention to you,
the foreign expert—but a man still stunned,
I knew, by the wild storks. *Tumult,* you said,

which took me, off-screen, nine words
to translate. Meanwhile the footage ran:
the hundred-year-old scaffolding on fire
beside the never-finished building—open,
always open, on top like an imperial vase.

Next, the parade's wrong turn into the dissident
district. Then the projectionist's error: pet bones
on a plate, cross-hatched in the zoom, divining sticks—
as if the future were being served up
in some soon-to-be-famous hot spot.

FRIDAY

Fish guts splayed across the dock.
A white cat drops a half-dead lizard
and steps out to lick them. Salt
brine. Not to eat but just to taste.

While the boats were at sea, a woman
told my fortune. Now she holds one end
of her husband's net, as he folds
the other—corner to corner.

My life is a full belly that doesn't
know it's full. Such was her verdict.
From her husband's hands the mesh
squares off and returns to her.

Her face wants me to believe the net is absolved
of all complicity. The lizard twists and bleeds
green across the sand. The woman kicks it
into the sea. And the froth mouth swallows.

JUMP SHIFT

The diplomat I'm supposed to be translating
suddenly switches languages on me. It's the third
time on this dream. String after string
of unrecognizable words. But he smiles. Nods.
And waits for me to translate. That's not
even a real language, I'm sobbing by the end.
That's nothing. Nothing! It's all made up.

NOSTALGIA

Happy walk: the girl going by
in a long blue skirt. Swishing.
Her hair whisked by her own
wind. I leave her behind:

in the square red brick buildings
of the Midwest, where people spoke
in hallways of the green knight, called him
Sir, were happy about his hardships.

The girl gone by: a brief breeze
through their buoyant talk,
and the sun all over her
as she dips her skirt among today's rustle.

Here, someone with her same name
misses her, leans back against
a red velvet chair—ripped and wobbly
from the last regime.

Later, in low wattage, I eat quail, finger
the topknot curled on a toothpick.
I feel the gone-girl frown up at this
through my smile. The table lamps

have that amber sheen, as in the time
when Christians were dipped in pitch
and burned. Sconces in the temples.
Emitting a warm glow, a steady light.

CAUTIONARY TALE

The funny bearded goat
goes down on his knees, the in-and-out
of frail ribs in the dust.

I listen, then tell you what the bellboy
said. Since he used his hands
I use mine. Since he's crying, I am.

The hotel's tiled lobby we'd walked through
yesterday—is today's dust around a goat.
All of us had been bussed to a basement.

Overhead, a factory of gray machines
and the ping-ping as metal parts shook loose.
Everyone gnawing at their own wounds

through a night of punctured breathing,
after a week of upended destinies,
and a long month between your dream

and mine. Keeping our distance,
and then not. The nuts and bolts
falling. I touched your chest.

Those ribs beneath your dusty suit
seemed the first ribs taking in
the first breaths of the world.

HE WANTS

He wants to stop and say we shouldn't be kissing like this, but he's already
entered the mouth of us, been hooked by and swirled through the O
of his own *No*. He wants to get out quick. Make amends. To see where
the sorrow is. The shame. The joy. He wants to ask about the storks
and their nests of opals atop the crumbling flown buttresses. About his wife
crying in France and telling their children it's only a low sun and the sting
of salt water and not to worry, It'll stop soon, it'll be all right.

He wants the soup of the turtle to arrive in its same shell but not
the grilled mackerel appearing with its head loose and eyes agog.
He wants to get over it. He wants what's already happened
not to. The space around him is his clothes and his children's faces—two boys
on a boat dock, casting. He wants back the space that is his, that he knows.
He wants the black socks in the black shoes to get up from the floor
and reclaim his delicate white feet. He wants to know what good, what good.

He wants to face the terminal where the computation of our days and deeds
goes green. Pulse and flick. Tick and beep. He wants to throw himself in front of
the two-ton, busted-brakes, 80% downhill grade of this kissing. The turtle's back
tells its story in reptilian code, which he wants the cryptographist in London
to crack in a hurry. He wants the buttons on my blouse to belong to the woman
he's still dreaming. He wants her to whisper, It'll be all right, all right? He wants
his fingers agile on those buttons, sleepily undoing what's already undone.

WHOEVER'S THE LAST BLESSED BLOWS OUT THE CANDLE

To hear a man laughing softly outside,
his face in my mind under those red maples.
To sit in the dark chapel and listen for a last
decibel of the laugh. Waiting it out.

And the stained-glass with a tiny white hole
in the blue hem of Christ's gown.
Everyone who sees it keeps its secret.

Remembering our driver's mother standing
this morning on the porchstep she'd just washed
as she does every day, and waving her wet rag
at us. Headed *Where,* she'd called,
though we'd only turned and nodded yes.

Outside the church, the plow horses drink slowly
from the new creek. A dirty water. Last week
when they'd pastured here, there'd been
no creek—the rain only light then. Cool
on their haunches. Today they nod up
those huge incredulous eyes, then nod
back down, drinking slowly, very slowly.

Dear Compatriots,

―――――◇―――――

if you put your finger on the map at Ouelseong
and let it twitch, you'll touch Driassa

which is where we are. Three boats tethered
to a set of old stone steps mark the town square.

Old women wring tattered flags over cobblestones.
A canal winds between lovely yellow buildings
that lean into each other's torsos.

A few tourists snap the boats' photo. No way
anywhere to phone anyone long distance.

Few police. Good coffee. All nine entryways
to the body have opened and buzz with traffic
during the dream: you expect to awaken
in another life in another place, where once
a bedsheet on a balcony meant surrender.

THE PLACE WE SHOULD NOT BE

Go north past the merman whose mouth once
spewed a geyser of water into the marble
fountain. Stripped now of the coins he can't spend,
he drips an old man's spittle. A spigot
left on, but no one knows where.

Hurry south of the fruitless fruit stalls
and meatless abattoir, where a young woman
sweeps nothing past the dust of nothing.
Past the pigeons and the filth. East
by the corpse and its attendant circle.

Step over the shattered glass into the garden.
It has a wind to lift my shirt. Fingers
of lily leaves. A way the body lies to itself,
claims No, you can't die here.

What touches us among the blossoms
are the thousand-storied clouds. We're well
west of a young man swimming to old age
in the canyons of the sea, miles beyond
the cyclone fence and sawhorse barricades,
the wet cigarette-butt and bullet-strewn alley.

When later I tell about the place we should not
have been, it will be as it was. Green
as it was. Green
as it is.

V

—◆—

SEEING ONESELF THROUGH THE EYES
OF THE BOY WHO BRINGS THE DRINKS

Ordering the cabbage soup, that wave of her hand.
Always a bit of drama where she goes.
Writing *pneumonia* in English, the rest in Cyrillic.
Her head on her hand over the *New York Times*
a week old already. Dancing with a married man
and trying to flirt in French. The sound of *her*
silver bracelets making this *her* kingdom.

Two turns of an antiquated key to open a door
just for a bed. Or later—after she's come to
under the raucous nymphs frescoed on the ceiling,
and the man's leaned into the pillows, sipped
what's left of the drink on the lace doily
and muttered, Someone is *always* sorry—finally
time to pull open the velvet curtains.

Moths fly out. The-Last-Alive is the dance they do.
Below, in the porte-cochère, bellboys smoke
under the No Smoking sign. She's bemused
by the one remaining Brezhnev in the plaza
who bobs on a balloon. Then someone buys him
and walks off with him. The seller folds up his stall
which becomes a bicycle that wheels itself away.

CELSIUS

Gold tassels shaking, the captain ordered an old man
        to go check the prayer books
on the stoop. Like steaks on a grill. Psalms
        in the sun. Tired of the flag and the flowers,
after a funeral people are thirsty. Tired of talking
        about failure. Pushing pins into maps.
A silver flask tips its hat over the coffee cups.

What they'd had for the coffin were two feet
        and a hand. Snow in my old city, but here
the sun pulses so hard, a tall building
        seems to bend. No sir, no heart in it,
the captain said. Part of the no-context I was
        used to. Taking cups to the kitchen
because the busboys were bombed.

You scowled, watching me. What string of lies
        the rest of our lives would have to live on
we'd begun to prepare. The parched mouths
        put by their manners. Sips gone to gulps, the flask
a jug. The box weighed next to nothing, I translated,
        loosely, on the porch where the prayer books
were stacked high and draped with lace hankies.

As Is His Wont

He wants to be brought back to himself. To lose himself. He wants it to be still early in the history of the world. And to reside right *here*, in this instant of passion transubstantiating itself into yet another democratic crusade.

He wants to feel bad and be left alone. To revel in the damp of me, the rain of my body dripping down. He wants his own country to get its affairs in order, and to understand how it possibly could. Without him.

He wants it to be an hour with heat and electricity humming, so he won't have to feel his way down rain-slick streets to our dark hotel where I won't be able to explain the pluperfect, and we'll both lie here, sleepless and confused about what was love and what is loyalty, and all for some country that doesn't know its own borders or even what its name on the new map will be.

He wants me to witness the dual question-marks of his shoulders walking away. To see him throw his hands down. To raise his hands up, as if to say Stop, *stop*. To shake out the shadows between our sentences and feel them drape. A cool on our heat. If only we could unload the dead fish from our dreams. If only what had been coming at us so fast—open-mouthed and already chewing—had frozen in its tracks, given us time to think it through, to think to think to think.

He wants back inside our endless passage: that processing of passion into its next declension. He wants the rain to quit. To have never begun. And for the sky to go on knotting and clenching, sending out spasms of voltage, thunder coughs, contortions—before its fissure rips open and the downpour pours down.

At the Higher Elevations

What's a thrill now but the taboo heights.
The snows of the peaks. The breaths
of a blizzard blowing. And greed, Madame,
greed. *God's hand hurts,* say the old women
we pass at the trailhead. We don't
follow this. They hate us. Fugitives
in thermal socks, we've flown in
from the future. They wear
black scarves. Peel potatoes.
Their hands hurt. They wave.

Everything Falls Away

The #86 train, its track, and
the track's gully down toward the sea, around
the mountain, and the mountain falling
rock by rock over the track, and across
my ancestors' lifetimes—before the gulls
and the Stark White Sand Ages
which fell away into the Gray Ages,
the Dark Ages. Sea of black
anonymity. Those gulls fall.
The civilized and the unfed, their cry
and feathers falling. First a tremble,
a wink of light, a blur. The slide
of your palms' warmth across my cool
hipbones. Down. Sea on a Sunday. Coffee
in tiny cups from the subdued life.
Slow gestures of the gulls,
top of the 6th on a radio, and
one man out. Heaps of the new world
around our feet, which we step out of
and fall away from too.

LOVING WHAT'S NEW

The guard's job is to protect the new waterpump
in the village. He chases away a boy who tries
to touch the long silver handle that glints—hot
in the sunlight. To touch it. Just for fun. It's not
a toy, the guard shouts, running, breathless.

In next week's photograph, the boy—with the pump
handle in his palm—lies blown maybe ten yards
from the pump itself, and from the boy's felt hat,
which we recognize, even upside-down in the rubble.
The handle shines like a stick of ice in the newsprint.

Not a toy. The boy had said, Yeah, he knew
that. But it made him smile to have it
finally in his hands. A small smile,
still half there on his half-face.

Watching the Men Walk

The man with the gold lighter lights five
tan cigarettes. Anoints the drizzle
with smoke. On his wrist: one watch
at 6 o'clock, one at 9:05.

And then the men walk. They walk
toward a mustard-colored building
where a band of boys sits on the roof
drinking the last of last year's vodka.
I raise my window to hear their toasts. Adieu
to the dregs of their country's potatoes.

The song from their boombox wafts off
into the smoke from five cigarettes
hovering over five new strategies.

The men in black wingtips glance up
at the wet young faces. Nod.
Who among us can help
but tap our toes, though it's a song
about the world's end.

Always Too Much and Never Enough

Out of bullets, the soldier impersonators
swung through town with antiquated swords
and scythes. The young news-hounds, tongues
dangling, rattled expensive pens, as on stage
and into a microphone, a man described
hammer blows to the head of his son.

In a bar, later, after sausages and dark beer,
he tells it again, more slowly, closing his eyes
this time around the hammer beats and his boy's
last breath. The man's sentences exactly the same,
but the rhythms changed, and his face,
and us leaning forward now and staring down
into his folding and unfolding hands to say No,
No, we've never heard such a terrible thing.

Portrait of the Lover with Eyes Closed

Darkly asleep in abundant daylight.
Toe by toe, sunlight striking your foot.

The pink tea proffered by our host at lunch
was a secret, he said—not to be told
to a woman, not to touch
her lips. Yet he needed mine
just to tell you that
as he put the cup of it—ground tiger
testicles—in your hand.

And now your closed eyes,
the quick toe-twitch
in afternoon twilight.

Because a peace was promised,
I shouldn't have been surprised
when you drank. Smiled and tipped
the cup. Though the peace
is still weeks of work
away. And, as always,
it'll wear off soon.

THE OLD HIGHWAY

: boot leather having worn its high spots low.
Fall-burnt sumacs are the bent, arthritic line
of old troops on review. The charmed life of the lie
ancient feet trod over
: reduced now to a tire-hum
through the old blood route.

          Only half there but thoroughly here
          with its missing chunks of stones.
          No longer traversable but we go
          down we go along we're in a hurry.

: all river shadow and river meandering.
The air above gains topography
from the gravel cut-work below.
A run-through of the Dardenelles.
Notched-up a knoll, a thimbleful
of compassion in the sunny dingle.

          Cloak of green opulence over
          a cityscape. Ride that around the defunct
          fountain. Reduced to lips and lips to
          what's shoved through and past them.

Powdery bones of the crooked cross-bow.
: a fist and a flag by the roadside. Heroes
of the great wars, helmets pulled low.

Below, a stadium full of lions. Above,
rooms in the inns for one's bad habits—
accommodations of absinthe, iced gin.

Making the pilgrimage to another body,
the anti-grail inside it and ready
to tip to shatter. Gone farther on what's here
there and half washed away.

The heroes' children having dropped their dolls
as breadcrumbs for the crows of history who bolt them
down. First, obsidian eyeballs, little porcelain skulls next,
and then those sumptuous bodies of dust.
The kisses of meeting and parting ruin
our mouths. A hard-pressed pleasure.

But it sets the pace. The scuffed byway,
a part of the pact that takes you apart.
When it's your turn you don't think you
just step up and duck out and go on along.

TO THE FAR NORTH

A plane aims toward the new moon,
which is luminous over us earthbound
sleepers. The sheen of worn spots
on our nightclothes. Bare ankles
in bare moonlight, where the dead
go searching for their living children—
dispersed now, far into the free provinces.

When I could not speak I gave you the tiny Chinese
fortune. From a cookie I could not eat.
A sentence of *Good highways ahead.* Kind words.
That scrap of white in your palm.
A patience to slow the failing light
as we stood to go separate ways. Kind
words. Few words. When we had none.

My language is a mist over the maize
back home. Neither these dead nor the living
know it. Here, words are cleaved
by coughs. A mouth of air, a blown lung.
And this clear frequency of moonlight.
Your plane's wild roar through my silence.

APPETITE. THE GREAT PAINTING.

The vulture ravishes a rabbit. Gold talons
grip the ripped chest, where the heart—
gloriously stroked by a few hairs—
appears still beating.

This is a country's masterpiece. Hauled in
and out of secret subterranean tunnels.
A viewer goes up close. As we did. The torn middle
is a mystery. Wounds on wounds.

The forest: all eyes in the background.
As we were in the foreground. Marvelous:
the high moon that gives no light.
The bird's beak and claws make their own.

Half-closed, the eyes of the one eating
have the look of a lover, loving.

Nance Van Winckel has published three collections of short stories and three previous collections of poems. She's the recipient of two National Endowment for the Arts Poetry Fellowships, the 1999 Washington Governor's Award for Literature, and the 1998 Patterson Fiction Award. She teaches in the graduate creative writing programs of Vermont College and Eastern Washington University.